GOLF SHOTS

How to Easily Hit a Wide Variety of Shots like Stingers, Flop Shots, Wet Sand Shots, and Many More for Better Scoring

Presented by The Team Golfwell

Published by: Pacific Trust Holdings NZ Ltd., 2017

This book contains Adult Golf Jokes and Adult Stories. ADULTS ONLY please.

Black and White Edition

You should always seek medical advice and/or check with your physician before doing the exercises and drills in this book or in any exercise program to avoid possible injury.

Praises received:

"This book helped me score better, and it's easier now to get the ball from Point A to Point B. Leaned a lot! Love the jokes too!"

- D. Higgins, Phoenix

"An excellent "How to Book". It's to the point and not complicated. And, entertaining! It makes the practice range more fun practicing these shots."

-J. Dennis, San Diego

"Liked the drills, jokes, and quotes. I've now got these shots in my game. I play faster, my scoring has improved. Makes range practice interesting rather than busting shots with the driver. Thanks!"

- S. Redmond, Naples, FL

"After reading about the various shots, I understand the whole game better now. I didn't notice the quiet subtleties of better scoring very well until I read this book giving me a wide variety of shots. They weren't hard."

-F. Davis, Sarasota, FL

Contents

PRACTICE TIP: *8*

INTRODUCTION *9*

SECTION ONE: TEE SHOTS............................*10*

....................*10*

1. THE STINGER..................................*12*

DRILL: How to Relax on the Tee *14*

2. DRAWING A TEE SHOT *16*

DRILL: Hit a Draw Tee Shot *18*

3. THE FADE *20*

DRILL: Hit a Power Fade Tee Shot *22*

4. LONGER DISTANCE TEE SHOTS: INCREASE YOUR "ANGLE OF ATTACK." 24

DRILL: Take Away Wide for More Length 27

5. USE ANY CLUB OFF THE TEE 28

6. DEALING WITH DIFFICULT TEE SHOTS 30

The Play Through Tee Shot 35

Distracted Driving 37

DRILL: Swing at 80% Power 39

Tee Shots with Homes Nearby 41

Borrow Your Driver Shot 41

Mulligans Off the First Tee Shot 43

Slices, Hooks, and Bad Tee Shots 43

SECTION TWO: APPROACH SHOTS 48

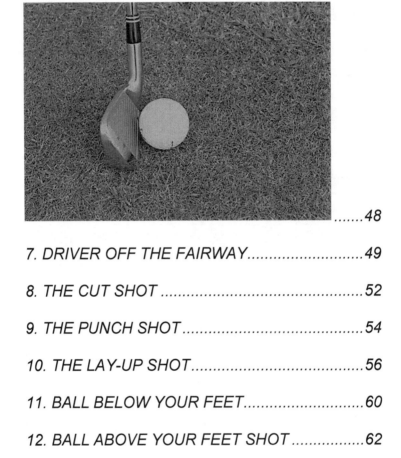

.......*48*

7. DRIVER OFF THE FAIRWAY............................*49*

8. THE CUT SHOT *52*

9. THE PUNCH SHOT *54*

10. THE LAY-UP SHOT...*56*

11. BALL BELOW YOUR FEET.............................*60*

12. BALL ABOVE YOUR FEET SHOT *62*

13. BALL ABOVE YOUR FEET - WITH YOUR FEET IN THE SAND AND VICE-VERSA..............*64*

14. RECOVERY SHOT..*66*

15. PLAYING SHOTS DOWN ANOTHER FAIRWAY..*69*

16. HITTING OUT OF A FAIRWAY DIVOT 73

17. HITTING OUT OF FAIRWAY BUNKERS 76

18. HITTING ON A DOWNSLOPE 79

19. HITTING ON AN UPSLOPE 81

20. HOW TO AVOID FAT SHOTS, THIN SHOTS, AND TOPPING THE BALL 82

21. HAVE NO FEAR OF ANY SHOT – HOW TO HIT HIGH OR LOW TRAJECTORY APPROACH SHOTS...84

Low and High Trajectory Shots.............................85

SECTION THREE: SHOTS AROUND THE GREEN 88

...................................88

22. LOB SHOT (FLOP SHOT) 90

23. PITCH SHOT *92*

24. CHIPPING...*94*

25. GREENSIDE BUNKER SAND SHOT.............*96*

Buried "Fried Egg" Bunker Shot............................*97*

Wet Sand Bunker Shots..*97*

26. FRINGE SHOTS *100*

27. CHIPPING FROM A DOWNHILL OR UPHILL SLOPE ONTO A FAST GREEN *103*

28. THE EASIEST SHOT IN GOLF *106*

29. THE DELICATE DROP SHOT.......................*109*

30. BUMP AND RUN SHOT *111*

31. HIT INTO THE BANK SHOT.........................*113*

DRILL: Hit Balls into the Bank............................*114*

"For the things we must learn before we can do those things, we learn them by doing them."

> *- Aristotle*

PRACTICE TIP:

For a more interesting practice session at the range, put this book on your phone or Tablet, or put it in your bag and take it to the range and practice the variety of golf shots featured in this book.

You will be a better and faster player and score much better.

INTRODUCTION

A good knowledge of shots enables you to quietly get the ball in the hole a lot easier. There are three sections in this book giving you a variety of shots for: 1. Tee Shots, 2. Approach Shots and, 3. Shots Around the Green.

This book is for all golfers, especially casual recreational golfers, to develop a wide variety of golf shots for better scoring.

Knowing how to do a variety of shots increases your ability to make better decisions on what shot to use to score better; and they're not hard to do.

We explain the various golf shots from the right-handed perspective (to avoid repetition) as left handers simply mirror these techniques to learn these shots.

We hope you enjoy this book and your golf becomes easier, your scoring gets better, and you have more fun playing!

SECTION ONE: TEE SHOTS

Photo Courtesy of Jeff Farsai, Jeff Farsai Photography, Long Beach

Having good tempo and being relaxed are two ways to have your muscles work naturally to allow the body to properly coordinate your golf swing.

Sergio Garcia said his philosophy in hitting tee shots is,

"When you make a few practice swings on the tee, think 'Tempo first.'"

Sergio said, "Notice I never make tee shots at full speed."

"I'll make a nice, controlled move, taking the club back and through."

"I'm not practicing for power, I'm practicing for balance."

As you read about the various tee shots (as well as approach shots and shots around the green) in this book, remember the importance of having good tempo and balance with every shot.

"The golf swing is very, very rhythmic."

"There's a certain tempo to it, just like in music."

- Justin Timberlake, Handicap Index 4.8

1. THE STINGER

"Every successful player has a shot they use and rely upon under intense pressure."

"My shot is a stinger or knockdown shot off the tee."

> *- Tiger Woods*

Tiger Woods likes the Stinger when he's under intense pressure. It's a low trajectory long distance with a three wood or long iron.

A Stinger is mainly used in windy conditions when you want the ball in the fairway. You simply play the ball further back in your stance – about one or two inches from where you normally tee it up.

You want the ball to fly on a low trajectory. So, play it back in your stance. Take an open stance with your left foot slightly turned out to help you make a shorter backswing.

Choke down on your club and swing smoothly concentrating on making good contact.

Use longer distance clubs from a 3 wood to a four iron. A high finish isn't necessary.

Of course, you must practice this shot. You'll find the time spent in practicing hitting a stinger will result in better scores especially when you want to be in the fairway and not searching for your ball in the rough.

*

"You need a good teacher that will keep the game fun and interesting for you."

"You have to work hard. Don't be afraid to have success one day and disappointment the next since that's golf."

- Paula Creamer

DRILL: How to Relax on the Tee

It's sometimes hard to relax on the tee when you deliberately want to relax.

If you're on the tee facing an intimidating tee shot, and taking several deep breaths and telling yourself "Just relax" isn't working, consider what Keegan Bradley suggests.

Keegan is an intense player. He believes it's best to keep your head clear and your body relaxed before hitting off the tee.

Keegan has said, "I focus on my facial muscles. I get my facial muscles to relax before hitting."

"When you can get your mouth to relax, your whole body relaxes."

Psychological studies have found that forcing your muscles to do something affects your mind and the way you think and feel.

Forcing a smile will make you happier.

In 1989, psychologist, Robert Zajonc studied whether forcing a smile actually makes you feel happier.

"When subjects tested made the "e" vowel sound and held the sound to make an "eee" sound, the subjects' face automatically smiled and felt happier."

"Similarly, when subjects make the "u" sound, and likewise held the "uuu" sound, the subjects automatically frowned and felt less happy."

Since then, it's been proven many times forcing a smile helps you relax and feel better. There is an article entitled, "Grin and Bear It: The Influence of Manipulated Positive Facial Expression on the Stress Response," in the Journal Psychological Science.

The Journal's website is: https://www.psychologicalscience.org/ and you can find the article there if you want to read further.

So, here's a Drill: to make yourself relaxed before you hit a tee shot, try relaxing your facial muscles.

2. DRAWING A TEE SHOT

There are golf courses favoring players who hit tee shot with a right to left draw. Bobby Jones designed Augusta that way.

Being able to hit a draw can dramatically reduce your score on a course favoring a right to left tee shot.

Drawn tees shots generally travel farther than faded tee shots.

There are two ways to hit a draw making the ball curve slightly from right to left off the tee:

1. Swing normally but close your clubface. The more you close your clubface the more draw you will have.

2. Swing normally and address the ball with a closed stance. Close your stance by dropping your

right foot back. The more your stance is closed, the more draw you will get.

Closing your club face and closing your stance will make the ball go right to left.

Again, keep good tempo and balance, and swing smoothly.

Practice the draw by closing your clubface and closing your stance on the range to get a feel for the amount of draw generated as you increase closing your clubface and stance.

Your closed clubface should be aligned to the right of your target.

You close your stance by dropping your right foot back, and your toe and shoulder line should be lined up further right of your target line, and further to the right of where your club face is pointing.

Take note of the amount of draw you generate as you close your stance and clubface in varying degrees, and find a position which makes you comfortable with the resulting draw.

*

Another way to hit a draw is to adjust your grip.

You adjust your grip to hit a draw by rolling your left hand over so you can see at least three knuckles on your left hand.

The crease in your right hand should point to your left shoulder (This is what is commonly called a "Strong Grip").

Then swing with your normal swing.

DRILL: Hit a Draw Tee Shot

At the range, pick a target directly ahead of you – i.e., straight ahead at the 12 o'clock position.

Place the ball on the tee with the brand of the ball (or a drawn straight line marked on the ball) pointing to your target at 12 o'clock.

If you want the draw the ball more from right to left, line up the brand of the ball (or the straight line drawn on the ball) to the 12:30 or 1:00 o'clock position.

Close your stance by dropping your right foot back lining up your body – toe and shoulder line -- with the brand or line on the ball pointing to the 1:30 or 2:00 o'clock position.

Align the club face to the 12:30 or 1:00 position, i.e., slightly to the right of your target.

Swing smoothly in your usual swing. Vary these positions to get comfortable with the amount of draw generated.

Tee off the left side of the tee box since it makes the fairway look much bigger. Also, it is easier from the left-hand side of the tee to start the ball down the right-hand side of the hole, and draw the ball back to the middle of the fairway (if the middle of the fairway is where you want your ball to land vs. the right or left side of the fairway).

3. THE FADE

"You can talk to a fade but a hook won't listen."

"Jack Nicklaus liked to curve the ball by opening or closing the clubface at address. I never felt I was good enough to do it his way."

"I didn't like changing my swing path, either, which some guys do. There's only one really reliable way to curve the ball: Change your hand position at address."

> *- Lee Trevino*

Just as there are golf courses favoring players who draw the ball of the tee, there are, of course, courses favoring players who fade the ball from left to right.

To hit a fade off the tee, you do the opposite of hitting a draw. There are two ways (combine both of them) to hit a fade off the tee are:

1. Swing normally but open your clubface. The more you open your clubface the more draw you will hit. You aim to the left of your target depending on the amount of fade you are going to hit.

2. Swing normally but address the ball with an open stance. The more your stance is open, the more fade you will hit.

Practice hitting a bucket on the range testing the fade by opening your clubface and by opening your stance.

When you open the clubface point the clubface at the target or slightly to the left of your target. Then open your stance so your shoulders and toe line are aimed further to the left than your clubface.

You can open your stance by advancing your right foot forward in your stance and turn your left foot slightly out. Align your toe and shoulder line to hit further to the left of your clubface.

There are other ways to hit a fade by adjusting your grip like Lee Trevino said.

You adjust your grip to hit a fade by rolling your left hand to the left and right hand to the right. You shouldn't be able to see knuckles on your left hand. You should only see knuckles on your right hand which should be covering your left thumb.

Lee Trevino, Tiger Woods and others use a power fade by holding the club with three fingers of their left hand to prevent the club face from closing right before striking the ball.

DRILL: Hit a Power Fade Tee Shot

At the range, pick a target directly ahead of you – i.e., straight ahead at the 12 o'clock position.

Place the ball on the tee with the brand of the ball (or line up a straight line marked on the ball) pointing to the 12 o'clock position.

If you want more fade, point the brand of the ball (or straight line marked on the ball) to the 11:00 or 11:30 o'clock position.

Open your stance by advancing your right foot forward and line up your toe and shoulder line pointing to the 10:00 or 10:30 o'clock position.

Point the club face to the 11:00 or 11:30 position, i.e., slightly to the left of your target.

Use your normal swing.

Tee the ball up on the right side of the tee and the fairway will look larger to you.

Practice fading the ball on the range by adjusting the amount of opening your clubface and opening toe and shoulder line in your stance. Your toe and shoulder line should line left of your target and left of your clubface.

*

"I'm a golfaholic."

"Counseling wouldn't help me."

"They'd have to put me in prison."

"Then I'd talk the warden into building me a hole or two."

"And, I'd teach him how to play."

> *- Lee Trevino*

4. LONGER DISTANCE TEE SHOTS: INCREASE YOUR "ANGLE OF ATTACK."

"What other people may find in poetry, I find in the flight of a good drive." - Arnold Palmer

Tee the ball forward from your usual position by teeing up 2 to 3 inches forward from your usual position. The reason you are doing this is to strike the ball with the face of your driver as it travels upward on the swing arc.

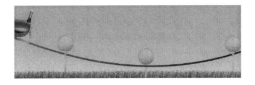

The further ahead you tee the ball up, the higher degree of your angle of attack.

Justin Thomas who hits it long for his 150 lb. 5 foot 9-inch frame consistently hits the ball at about a 5-degree angle of attack which causes the ball to fly high, i.e. the old saying, "Tee it high and let it fly."

To hit it long, avoid over swinging - just swing at your normal speed and focus on making good contact rather than swinging hard. The physics of the angle of attack will do the rest.

To do this simply, take a normal stance, or even a wider stance to help your stability.

The ball teed forward may look odd to you. But disregard the position of the actual ball teed forward.

Instead, imagine a ball is teed up in the normal position where you usually tee it up (e.g., off your left heel) and imagine you are looking at the back of the imaginary ball positioned off your left heel.

Make a smooth swing, disregarding the actual ball is teed up further ahead 2-3 inches. Your club will do the rest.

*

Another method of hitting it longer is the method Jason Day uses.

Jason is a long hitter and uses "Imaginary railroad tracks" to help him make a wide arc on driving the ball to generate more power."

Keep in mind, Jason is not swinging harder. His use of a wide arc makes the clubhead travel faster when Jason swings at his normal tempo or even a slower tempo.

Jason, "Visualizes the clubhead above the outside rail of railroad track and his hands are above the lower rail."

"I take away my hands and clubhead in one piece creating a wide swing arc."

"The wider the arc, the more power I generate."

DRILL: Take Away Wide for More Length

Tee the ball up and imagine the clubhead of your driver is aligned and parallel on the top rail of a railroad track and your hands are aligned with the bottom rail.

The rails of the railroad track point in the direction of your target, i.e. the area where you want your drive to land on the fairway.

Practice a short takeaway by bringing the driver head back to the 3 o'clock position keeping your left and right arm straight until you reach the 3 o'clock position with your arms.

Your hands and clubhead should travel parallel on the tracks as you take your clubhead to the 3 o'clock position.

Repeat this takeaway until it feels comfortable.

Then do several full swings.

Keep in mind you shouldn't try to swing harder. Instead you are focusing on making good contact with the ball.

Keep hitting balls to grove this swing and wide arc high club head speed shot.

5. USE ANY CLUB OFF THE TEE

"Most all of us feel nervous over an opening tee shot. But thinking about being nervous is a deterrent to success.... So, don't wonder about it since it's no benefit to you. It is "Fearful Golf" when what success demands is "Fearless Golf."

> *- Dr. Gio Valiante*

The rules of golf allow you to use any club in your bag off the tee. Jack Nicklaus possessed excellent course management abilities and used his three-wood off the tee more often than he used his driver.

"You know what they say about big hitters...the woods are full of them."

> *- Jimmy Demaret*

It's better to make the green on a long par 4 in three shots compared to spending time looking for a lost ball in the rough and then having to play your provisional.

Also, if there are undulating areas you would most likely hit to using your driver, it's better to hit shorter to a flat area where your second shot is easier to hit off level ground.

If you take a long iron or hybrid off the tee, don't try to scoop it or help the ball into the air, rather let the club do that.

Tee the ball up about a ¼ inch off the ground if you're using a long iron.

As you go up in irons off the tee (say a 5 iron) tee the ball closer to the ground since you don't want to hit the ball toward the top of the iron blade which will cost you distance.

Make a nice wide takeaway with a long iron and make a smooth swing.

6. DEALING WITH DIFFICULT TEE SHOTS

The next tee shots may create negative thoughts. Here's suggestions on how to deal with them.

Prevent Slow Play from Ruining Your Shots

Rickie Fowler said,

"It's harder to score well in a slow round. The tendency is to overthink shots while you're waiting and become mentally exhausted."

Rickie suggested a remedy:

"Instead of overthinking a shot, chat with your playing partners about anything but golf. Concentrate on each shot for no more than a minute."

"You'll stay fresh this way."

If your foursome is experiencing slow play, take practice swings as well to keep yourself loose, of course.

Here's some other shots and situations:

The Whiff or Air Shot

(and its consequences)

Even PGA Tour Players whiff the ball (sometimes called an "Air shot") attempting a drive.

Kevin Na looked like he whiffed a tee shot while millions of viewers watched in the third round of a PGA Tour Tournament.

But, what clearly looked like a whiff was ruled no whiff since the official concluded he wasn't intending to hit the ball, even though many viewers disagreed.

So, what looked like a clear whiff wasn't counted as a stroke. Keven went on the next day to win the tournament.

Rory McIroy whiffed a chip.

A whiff occurs more frequently where a Tour player whiffs a 1 or 2-inch putt not paying attention to tapping it in. Everyone gets annoyed at barely missing a putt. The tendency is to walk fast up to

31

the ball on the edge of the cup and tap it in. This is where most whiffs occur.

Any attempt to hit the ball counts as a stroke. If you are on the tee and whiff the ball, it counts as a stroke.

If your ball is still on the tee, you can stay on the tee and hit it again, but it's now your second shot. That is, you don't have to let the others in your group tee off and then play your second shot.

If the speed of your swing missing the ball blows the ball off the tee, you must hit your second shot where the ball lies – can't retee it without taking a penalty stroke.

So, if you retee it, you are replaying the ball and have to take a one stroke penalty so you are now hitting three.

Once you whiff a tee shot, you'll be under a bit more pressure from the rest of your foursome. It's common to hear someone call out, "One!" after you whiff it.

(There's a "Whiff the Tee Off Joke" at the end of this chapter to help you laugh it off and relax if you do whiff a tee shot.)

If you dig your club into the tee box turf behind the ball without hitting it, and the ball remains on the tee, that's a stoke, since you attempted to hit the ball.

If you stop your swing before you hit the ball off the tee, that doesn't count as a stroke. You may have seen PGA Tour Players stop their swing on the downswing, step back and go through their pre-shot routine again without incurring a penalty.

A whiff, as well as topping the ball off the tee, can be due to moving or lifting your head during the swing.

To prevent your head from moving during your swing, keep your back straight and slightly bent forward at the hips, i.e., take the stance of a linebacker and let gravity pull your arms so they hang straight down from your body perpendicular to the ground.

Also, focus on the back of the ball, instead of the top of the ball. When you focus on the top, you tend to hit down on the ball when driving a ball off the tee.

Focusing on the back of the ball tells your mind to tell your body to sweep the ball off the tee instead of lifting up and hitting down on it at a steep angle.

*

"A Whiff Off the First Tee"

It's Sunday morning and 4 guys are waiting to tee off on the first tee, but there are four ladies in a group in front of them waiting to tee off at the lady's tee. The ladies are talking away oblivious to everything.

The fairway became clear a few minutes ago, but the ladies are still gabbing away.

One of the men loudly clears his throat to get their attention.

The ladies turn around to look at the man, and he is now politely pointing down the open clear fairway.

Three of the ladies quickly hit their tee shots, but the fourth woman slowly parades up to the tee, takes fifteen practice swings then whiffs her tee shot. Red-faced, she tries to hit it again, but only dribbles it off the tee.

She turns to the 4 men behind her and says, "I'm sorry. All those fucking lessons I took this winter didn't help me a bit."

One of the men says, "Oh, I understand your problem, you should have been taking golf lessons instead."

The Play Through Tee Shot

"The greatest efforts in sports come when the mind is as still as glass."

- W. Timothy Gallwey

You are first player of your group to tee off and you notice the foursome in front searching the rough halfway down the first fairway.

One of them looks back at you on the tee, and waves you and your group through.

You wave back acknowledging the courtesy.

Even though you know you don't have to hurry, some players want to play quicker when asked to play through.

So, you do your pre-shot routine to forget about the additional people watching you.

You know you don't have to rush. But, your mind is telling you you've been in this play-through situation before, and rushed your tee shot - dribbling it off the tee and embarrassed yourself.

Former US Open Champion, Graeme McDowell has said,

"You turn off your mind."

"You feel your golf swing without really thinking about it."

"It's almost like you don't think at all."

"Maybe you have one little thought, and everything else becomes automatic."

If you can't turn off your mind, try having only one thought in your mind like the thought of making a smooth swing. And, don't forget to simply step away if there are too many thoughts going on in your brain.

Do a pre-shot routine before you hit your playing through tee shot. Tell yourself, you're going to have an enjoyable round and you are happy to know you won't have this group holding you up for the round.

Also, realize it really doesn't matter how you hit the ball, just think about making a smooth swing as Jack Nicklaus said,

"I've always thought the phrase 'hit it nice and easy' when a golfer needed a big shot, was dopey advice. 'Hit it nice and smoothly' sounds much better to me."

Dustin Johnson believes staying on an even keel is more important than playing well or playing bad (as he demonstrated when he was told he was penalized a few holes back for moving the ball with his putter during the final round of the 2016 US Open).

Dustin has said,

"I try not to get too emotional, whether it's going really well or going really bad, I always try to stay on an even keel -- which is great for golf, but it isn't always great for life."

When you are asked to play through, try to turn off your mind as Graeme McDowell suggests, or, at most, have only one swing thought.

Distracted Driving

If you get distracted while you a preparing to hit a tee shot, keep things simple, even though some of the following events occur:

1. The pretty refreshment card girl mistakenly drives up while you are ready to hit your drive.

2. There's a water hazard on the hole which requires a 200-yard carry and you hear mumblings behind you, "He's going swimming."

3. You're playing with your boss. He's just had a bad hole, and he's annoyed at you for some unknown reason.

4. There is any other distraction, e.g., cell phone going off, unexpected sounds, etc.

First, in order to relax, try to understand your own feelings which might be:

1. You want to impress the cart refreshment girl, and you don't want to look stupid.

2. You're worrying about the water hazard.

3. You're miffed but you know you haven't done anything to make your boss upset. You understand he will calm down with his annoyance in his own time and you are going to let him calm down by himself.

4. Distractions annoy you, but they happen.

Understanding your own feelings has a calming effect on yourself.

Nick Faldo suggests in distracting situations, to keep your swing and thoughts simple. Nick has said to make the golf swing simple just, "Sit, coil, pull, and release."

Faldo suggests using no more than 80% of your power when you don't feel comfortable.

When Faldo was learning golf, he was taught a routine to try and hit an iron with only 50% of his power and then gradually work his way up to hitting it with 80% of his power.

"Golf confidence is being able to concentrate on the problem at hand with no outside interference."

- Tom Watson

DRILL: Swing at 80% Power

When you're at the range, try hitting a few balls swinging as hard as you can. Turn up the tempo of your swing to 110%+.

It doesn't matter if you hit the ball or not, just experience your quickest swing.

Then, hit the next ball as easily as you can (using the least amount of power you have) and work your way up to hitting it with 50% of your power.

Then, gradually increase the tempo of your swing from 50% up to around 80% of your power.

When you are up to hitting at a tempo of 80% continue hitting using an 80% tempo (no more – no less).

Many recreational golfers try to force a shot to happen, especially over a water hazard or any other type of hazard.

The great Byron Nelson said, "Get rid of the forced shot. The only thing you should force in a golf swing is the club back in the bag."

Know the golf swing generates a lot of force to send a 1.620-ounce (45.93 gram) golf ball flying. Extra force isn't necessary.

Forcing a shot causes your muscles to tense up as your body subconsciously tries to force the blade of the club to hit the ball harder. Or, to "steer" a shot.

So, think, "Keep it simple" any time you begin to overthink a shot. Relax and hit your tee shot with an 80% tempo and only focus on making good contact.

"In character, in manner, in style, in all things… the supreme excellence is… simplicity."

- Henry Wadsworth Longfellow

Tee Shots with Homes Nearby

Breaking a window, or damaging a home, etc. are additional costs of playing a course in a housing development.

If you want to hit it straight, Adam Scott has a suggestion when you want to get rid of negative thoughts creeping into your head.

Adam has said, "Whatever I'm working on, I like to keep one swing thought in my head when I'm on the course."

"Keeping it simple helped me at the Deutsche Bank Championship in Boston."

Adam said, "Thinking only about getting to my left side, I shot 62 Friday and won the Deutsche Bank event."

If you ever have too many thoughts creeping in, remember what Adam Scott does – just try to keep only one thought in your mind.

Borrow Your Driver Shot

May I try your driver?"

In casual recreational play, friends borrow each other's clubs to try them out. Especially after someone has a new driver.

Rule 4-4a doesn't allow you to borrow clubs from another player, except if it's your partner and you can share clubs with your partner. But you are only allowed to share clubs with your partner where the total number of clubs carried in your bag and your partner's bag does not exceed 14.

If you and your partner have more than 14 clubs combined, there is a two-stroke penalty in stroke play.

In casual recreational play, foursomes ignore this rule since people are curious when a member of their foursome has a new club, especially a driver.

But, an agreed waiver of a rule of golf is a violation of the rules of golf as well under Rule 1-3.

In any event, when you buy a new driver, you know the others will want to try it.

Most of us have no problem sharing, and most club borrowers are responsible and know they may be crossing a line by asking to try a shiny new driver.

If you share, just tell the borrower, "Give a try, but you pay for a new one if you nick it or break it."

Mulligans Off the First Tee Shot

Rules of golf don't allow mulligans, of course.

If you do allow mulligans in casual play, make sure everyone in your group clearly understands what the "Mulligan Rules" are.

For example, you hit a short drive about 90 yards and then elect to use your mulligan to get the ball out to where you usually hit it. You then hit the mulligan drive out of bounds.

Can you take back to your first drive? Some golfers say if you play a mulligan, you must continue to play the mulligan ball and you can't go back to your first ball.

Generally, the best way to handle this, is to clarify with everyone before you start whether you can play your first ball even if you use a mulligan.

Slices, Hooks, and Bad Tee Shots

"To avoid a hook, my takeaway thought is to make sure during those first three feet the clubhead works away wide and outside my hands, with a nice bit of loft on the club."

- Rory McIroy

Let's start by discussing a slice since it's very common. A slice (which is a severe left to right curve) can be cause by several things:

First, by a very weak grip - which is having your left hand turned far to the left so you're unable to see the knuckles on your left hand, and you strike the ball with an open club face.

Or, your toe line and shoulders are aimed too far left. In other words, your right foot is forward in your stance creating an open stance, and your club face is aligned straight ahead, or way to the right of where your toe line and shoulders are pointing.

Or, a slice can be caused by an outside to inside swing which creates a fast-clockwise spin on the ball causing it to sharply curve to the right.

We all know if you're hitting into a wind, the amount of curve will increase proportionately to the strength of the wind, i.e. the stronger the wind, the more it will curve when hitting into a strong wind.

The more you aim to the left with your toe line and shoulder line, and the more you aim the club face to the right of your toe line and shoulders, the more you will to slice the ball to your right.

To stop the slice and hit a nice fade, try the drill in Chapter 3. Or, try taking a neutral grip, or even a strong grip. Check the alignment of the club face of your driver and straighten or close the club face and/or your stance more.

*

If you want to hit a severe slice intentionally, use a weak grip, put your right foot forward, have your toes and shoulders lined up way to the left of your target, and your club face lined up to the right of your target.

If you want to severely hook the ball intentionally, do the opposite:

To hook the ball, use a very strong grip, and align your club face to the right of your target. Then drop your right foot far back so you have your toe line and shoulder lined up even further to the right of your target.

The more you aim to the right of your target with your toe and shoulder line and the more you close your clubface, the more you will to hook the ball.

*

If you just unintentionally sliced, or hooked a ball, or, if you just hit a terrible drive, don't let your mind beat you up.

Visualize your next shot while you are calming down. Take deep breaths and realize that visualizing your next shot, and doing your pre-shot routine before you hit your next shot, will put you in the present. You will forget about the past – which you, of course, can't change anyway.

Rory McIroy has said when he feels pressure, he does one simple thing,

"I pick a spot a foot in front of the ball and focus on swinging my club over the spot. The ball will be hit automatically. That takes my mind off the outcome of the shot and keeps me in the present."

Confidence helps a great deal in executing a tee shot, as well as the entire game of golf.

Sam Snead had more confidence than most golfers. Sam once said, "Could I have whipped Tiger Woods? Hell, yes.... No man scared me on the golf course."

Before any tee shot, or any shot in golf, be it a booming drive or a tap in putt, keep your confidence at a good level.

Before a round of golf, an important meeting, a job interview, a date with the beautiful woman, or whatever, tell yourself you are absolutely not going to criticize yourself for anything. You are going to stay positive and be as positive as you can no matter what.

It's been said many times, Confidence is the foundation for success in life and achievement.

Instead of criticizing yourself, think of all the good and great things you have done to get to the opportunity you are experiencing now.

"When a player is silently waiting his turn to hole out a putt of one or two feet in length, and the entire match hangs on him making the putt,"

"It is of vital importance that he thinks of nothing."

"He ought to fill his mind with vacancy. He must not even allow himself the consolation of religion."

- Sir Walter Simpson (The Art of Golf)

SECTION TWO: APPROACH SHOTS

"I can still see the shape of the shot in my mind when looking down at the ball."

-Tiger Woods

7. DRIVER OFF THE FAIRWAY

"Your next shot is a new experience. It might be the best shot you ever hit in your life."

- Harvey Penick

If your driver has at least 10.5 degrees loft, and you practiced this shot and feel confident hitting a driver off the fairway, then more power to you to add this shot to your golfing ability.

Hitting a driver off the fairway with less than 10.5 degrees of loft is difficult due to the physics involved.

To hit a ball off the fairway with a driver, play the ball more forward in your stance from where you normally hit a driver off the tee.

The shot is easier when the ball is on an upslope and sitting up high on the turf.

Choke up on the driver if you have a shaft longer than 43.5 inches. Tiger Woods normally uses a 43.5-inch shaft and your chances of hitting the ball on the sweet spot increase as you decrease the length of the shaft.

The ball will roll more, so hit driver off the fairway where there are no hazards or traps the ball can roll into along the hitting line to your target.

Stand more upright (than you would as if hitting off the tee) to make it easier to make a downward swing at the ball.

Don't try to force the ball into the air. Swing smoothly and concentrate on making solid contact with the back of the ball, rather than swinging fast or hard.

You use a downward swing (imagine you are going to take a small divot), as this will help you have more solid contact with the ball.

On the negative side, a driver off the fairway is a high risk shot for the average recreational golfer.

Driving off the tee is a lot different from hitting driver off the fairway. You may be an excellent driver off the tee, but that doesn't mean you are going to have an easier time hitting driver "Off the deck."

When you hit off a tee you are swinging <u>up</u> at the ball. When you hit driver off the fairway, you must hit <u>down</u> at the ball.

"You have to be precise when you hit driver off the fairway, but it's not impossible."

"It takes precision."

"But the shot is easier than it was five years back since a lot of new driver heads have a lower center of gravity."

> *- Rickie Fowler*

8. THE CUT SHOT

A cut shot is a good approach shot since it has backspin plus additional side spin. Because of the trajectory and spin, a cut shot tends to hold the green better than a ball being drawn in from right to left to the green.

Use a weak grip, and open the club face.

Address the ball with an open stance and use your normal swing.

The club face should be lined up to the left of the target, and your toe and shoulder line aimed further left of your target depending on how much you want the ball to curve to the right.

A cut shot is useful in getting around objects vs. hitting away from your target line. If it's a windy day, take into account the wind direction and make allowances for the strong winds to exaggerate or diminish the left to right curve of the ball.

When you hit a cut shot, you don't want to close the face of the club, as you want to make contact with the ball with an open club face. After you strike the ball on your downswing, make an underhand motion with your right hand as you come up on the ball and continue the underhand motion as you follow through. This will keep the club face open creating a left to right spin on the ball.

When you finish the underhand motion swinging through, your right palm should be facing upward toward the sky on your follow through.

If the club face should close before you impact the ball, you will hit the ball too far to the left and it won't spin it enough to curve back to your target.

"Golf is a game that's mind boggling. Can't figure out. One day you shank shots, slice shots, hit into every trap, and miss every green."

"The next day you go out and, for no reason at all, you're really lousy at it."

-Bob Hope

9. THE PUNCH SHOT

"One shot that I use in windy conditions to keep my golf round under control is the low knock down punch shot."

- Justin Rose

A punch shot or "knock down" shot keeps the ball in a low trajectory and is commonly used in windy conditions, or hitting under tree branches or other obstacles.

Use one or two clubs more than you usually use considering the strength of the wind and distance to the target.

Play the ball slightly back your stance and because you are playing the ball back in your stance, your hands will be slightly forward of the golf ball.

Put 60% of your weight on your left side. Your right shoulder should be a bit higher than your normal stance position.

Use a shorter backswing and a shorter follow through, and use more of your arms. Since you are using more of your arms to hit the ball, there isn't much of a weight transfer and this is another reason you need to use more club than usual.

Swing at normal speed focusing on making good contact.

The trajectory of the ball should be about half of your normal trajectory.

Overall, the punch shot is a fairly simple shot to execute and very helpful in windy conditions.

"In golf, as it is in life, you've got to outthink and be prudent to handle bad weather, or anything stronger than you can control, to avoid being blown away."

> *- Anon.*

10. THE LAY-UP SHOT

You find yourself on a long par 5, or a long par 4 and you have a very long shot (say 250 yards) to reach the green in regulation.

Ask yourself, "What is the longest club I can hit with the most accuracy?"

You determine, you can reliably hit your 5 wood or hybrid to an area 75 to 60 yards from the green.

You also need to consider your next shot after that. If you are more comfortable hitting to the green from 100 yards rather than 60 to 75 yards, consider hitting a shorter club to an area 100 yards away rather than 75 to 60 yards away.

Whatever you determine, then decide on a specific area to hit to. This will make your shot easier and your mind will coordinate your body to make the shot exactly to the specific area you want your ball to land.

Jack Nicklaus said it's very important to pick a specific area to hit to,

"I never hit a shot, not even in practice, without first having a very sharp, focused picture of the shot in my head."

"It's like a color movie."

"First, I 'see' where I want the ball to finish, nice and high, and sitting up high on green grass."

"Then the scene quickly changes."

"Next, I 'see' the ball going there: its path, trajectory, and its shape."

"Even its behavior on landing."

"Then there is sort of a fade-out."

"In the next scene, I see myself making the kind of swing that makes it all a reality."

Lay up shots are useful to avoid trouble and occasional use of lay up shots shows you have good course management awareness.

You don't always have to clear the hazard and generally, it's better to play smart than try to play above your normal ability.

Lay up shots are also used to position the ball making your shot to the pin easier.

For example, when a pin is tucked on the right side of the green just behind a large deep bunker, you can play a lay-up shot to a point in front of the green where you can chip cleanly to the pin without any trouble in the line to the pin.

*

A golfer stumbles and bumbles through the door of his house several hours late and his wife greets him at the door with an ominous look he's all too familiar with.

"Where the hell were you?"

Exasperated, the golfer throws his arms up in the air and says,

"I'm sorry, Honey."

"Don't 'Sorry' me, you bastard!"

"Okay, okay…the truth shall set me free…," he mumbles to himself, then says,

"I just finished my round and was putting my clubs in the trunk when I noticed a young beautiful woman fumbling by her car trying to fix her own flat tire. I offered to help her and… I changed her tire."

"Go on," said the wife tapping her foot sternly.

"She thanked me again and again, and we kept talking then we went to a bar. The next thing I know I'm in bed with her at her place. Then I fell asleep for a while and came right home. I'm so sorry, honey, can you find it in your heart to forgive me?"

The wife stared at him, "Don't you give me that shit, you played 36 holes today, didn't you!"

"A 'Great Shot' is when you pull it off."

"A 'Smart Shot' is when you don't have the guts to try it."

> *-Phil Mickleson*

11. BALL BELOW YOUR FEET

When the ball is below your feet, you risk hitting it thin since the ball is vertically further away from you.

You need to keep your balance and make good contact when you hit the ball.

Gravity also wants to pull you down the slope of the hill in the direction of the slope.

So, to keep yourself properly balanced with the ball below your feet, you need to "sit down" a bit more than normal, and flex your knees more. Your weight should be in your heels instead of the balls of your feet.

Take a wider stance than you usually do as this tends to lower your body and help you keep good balance when striking the ball.

Stand nearer to the ball. This, in effect, makes your club longer and making good contact with the ball is easier.

Aim left of your target, since hitting a ball below your feel will automatically create a left to right fade. The further you are away from your target, the more your ball will fade.

And, the steeper the slope downward, the more your ball will fade.

Alignment is very important with approach shots, and makes a big difference in your game.

Make a smooth swing with good tempo at your target.

"It goes without saying, that it's no good having a perfect set up, a perfect grip, and a perfect golf swing if the whole thing is misaligned."

"Many players don't spend enough time getting themselves on target."

- Nick Faldo

12. BALL ABOVE YOUR FEET SHOT

When the ball is above your feet, choke up on the club. The higher the ball is from the bottom of your feet, the more you choke up on your club.

Otherwise, you risk chunking the shot and hitting it fat.

The steeper the slope the more you should aim to the right of your target because the ball will naturally go from right to left.

You can consider standing more erect. However, keep in mind, the more erect you stand, your swing becomes flatter which will make your hands turn over and pull the ball even more to the left.

The steeper the slope and the greater the distance to your target, the more draw you will have curving the ball to the left of your target. So, make sure to allow for the automatic draw that comes with hitting a ball on an uphill slope.

If you want to reduce the amount of the draw, you can try opening your clubface more to counteract the draw.

If you are on a very steep slope, put your weight on the balls of your feet to help keep your balance when striking the ball.

Also, take a wider stance and get yourself comfortable and balanced.

Focus on making good contact. Consider using only 75%, or less, of your normal tempo to make it easier to make good contact. If you decide to swing easier, take more club.

"No matter how terrible you are playing, even if it's the worst round in your life, keep in mind it can always get worse."

> *- Anon.*

13. BALL ABOVE YOUR FEET - WITH YOUR FEET IN THE SAND AND VICE-VERSA

If your ball is above your feet but in the fairway, and your feet are in a fairway bunker, keep in mind you won't be able to use your legs as you normally do. You'll be mainly swinging with your arms. This will decrease the distance you hit the ball.

If you're not able to reach the green, use good course management and lay up.

If your ball is below your feet in a sand trap, and you are standing on the grass to the side of the sand trap, you need to set yourself up as you would if you making a golf shot with the ball below your feet as explained in Chapter 11.

Flex your knees more to lower your club to where you will make solid contact with the ball.

Your swing should not come down at the ball at a steep angle as you risk catching too much sand. A steep swing at the ball could drive the ball into the sand.

You will strike the ball more consistently if you pick it clean off the sand with a shallow swing coming in at a shallow angle rather than a steep angle.

*

It's been said, the game of golf may cause brain damage:

At a very exclusive golf course in Scotland, a very wealthy and eccentric golfer walked to the first tee accompanied by two caddies - one carrying his clubs and the other carrying a large plush couch.

The Starter stopped him, "Sir, you aren't allowed to bring two caddies on this course. And, I cannot imagine you would have that other poor man lug your couch around this course. Not a good look, sir."

The golfer replied, "Oh, that's not my caddy. He, sir, is my psychiatrist."

14. RECOVERY SHOT

A recovery shot is any imaginable way of getting your golf ball out of trouble.

The ball could be in deep rough, heavy bushes, up in a tree, slightly submerged in a water hazard, against a natural object, etc.

Before deciding to hit a recovery shot, you should feel confident you can make good contact with the ball to have it travel the necessary distance so you are able to hit your next shot well.

You need to determine how you're going to do it, and be reasonably sure you can play it out of trouble to an area where you could hit a good shot.

Otherwise, consider taking an unplayable lie with a one-stroke penalty and move on.

Probably Bubba Watson made the most well-known recovery shot out of trees in the 2012 Masters on 10th hole.

When Bubba hit his drive deep into the trees, most everyone gave up on Bubba doing well. Then he spectacularly hooked the ball onto the green.

There are ways to get a free drop when you're in deep rough. For example, if you feel threatened because of a hornet's nest, a red ant hill or anything else which would reasonably threaten you, you are allowed a free drop.

Be aware of local rules. Some courses allow a free drop if your swing might damage a nearby sapling tree under 6 feet.

Or, look for any "Abnormal ground conditions" which might entitle you to a free drop.

Playing left handed recovery shots, or any unorthodox shot should be avoided unless you feel reasonably confident you can pull it off.

If you decide to play a recovery shot, focus on making good and clean contact with your club to the back of the ball to hit it far enough to an area that will give you an easier next shot.

*

Two golfers were playing a South African jungle golf course on a summer's day.

One of the golfers hooked his ball into the thick jungle foliage which disappeared into thick greenery and down a steep bank into a dense jungle ravine.

He grabbed a sand wedge and went down the slope in search of his ball. He searched and searched, noticing several large buzzards circling above him.

The sound of large snakes slithering through the deep grass filled his ears, as well as the sound of menacing jungle animals gradually moving away from him as he continued his search.

As he parted several branches of a large bush, something sparkled from the ground that caught his eye.

He looked closer and saw the shining object was an old sand wedge in the hands of a skeleton lying on the ground next to an old yellowed golf ball.

He spotted his own ball about a foot away from the skeleton.

He shouted out to his partner, "Joe, come here. I've got some *serious* trouble down here."

"What's the trouble?" Joe asks.

"Bring me my pitching wedge. You can't get out of here with a sand wedge!"

15. PLAYING SHOTS DOWN ANOTHER FAIRWAY

If you slice or hook your tee shot onto an adjacent fairway, consider playing the ball down the other fairway.

Many players feel they must hit the ball back onto their own fairway; but if it's legal to play it down an adjacent fairway, do so if it makes the hole easier for you.

Be mindful of local rules as well as staked OB markers which would not allow you to hit a ball from an adjacent fairway.

If you play it down on an adjacent fairway, hit it to the green when you can, or lay up – whatever you feel is best.

Don't feel embarrassed playing down an adjacent fairway. Everyone has done it if it's legal to do so.

It's good to be mindful of this option if it makes the hole easier to play.

*

A Blonde on an Adjacent Fairway

A blonde hooked her ball and splashed it into a river running along the left side of the hole. The deep river also separated the fairway from an adjoining fairway.

The blonde went to see if she could retrieve her ball out of the river. She saw her ball near the other side of the river, but couldn't reach it even with her fully extended ball retriever.

She thought and thought, but just couldn't figure out how to cross the river to get to the other side where she could easily get her golf ball.

Another lady (also blonde) came up to her ball on the other side of the river. The other blonde smiled and waved to the blonde whose ball was in the river.

"How do I get to the other side?" said the blonde who hit her ball into the river.

"You're already on the other side," said the other blonde.

More jokes here

16. HITTING OUT OF A FAIRWAY DIVOT

If your ball comes to rest in a fairway divot, the rules require you to play the ball as it lies. You can't move it.

If the divot is very deep, consider taking an unplayable lie with a one stroke penalty.

If the ball comes to rest in a divot that's not filled with sand, and you believe you can play the ball, play the ball back in your stance so your club will make good contact with the ball.

Keep in mind, if the divot is deep, you play the ball out of the divot swinging in the direction of the divot with a wedge or other high lofted club even though that may not be the direction you want to go.

If the ball comes to rest in a sand filled divot and the divot runs in the direction of your target, you can play the ball out like a fairway bunker shot by picking it clean off the sand.

Take an extra club, since you will be swinging mainly with your arms to keep your lower body steady, and play the ball back in your stance with your hands ahead of the ball. Put slightly more weight on your front foot.

Commit yourself to the shot and make a smooth swing and focus on picking the ball cleanly off the sand.

Picking the ball off the sand is more fully explained in the next chapter.

*

Here's an argument to make golf courses more natural:

"Golf epitomizes the tame world."

"On a golf course nature is neutered. The grass is clean, a lawn laundry that wipes away the mud, the

insect, the bramble, nettle and thistle, an Eazy-wipe lawn where nothing of life, dirty and glorious, remains."

"Golf turns outdoors into indoors, a prefab mat of stultified grass, processed, pesticided, herbicided, the pseudo-green of formica sterility."

"Here, the grass is not singing. The wind cannot blow through it. Dumb expression, greenery made stupid, it hums a bland monotone in the key of the mono-minded."

"No word is emptier than a golf tee. No roots, it has no known etymology, it is verbal nail polish."

"Worldwide, golf is an arch act of enclosure, a common fenced and subdued for the wealthy, trampling serf and seedling."

"The enemy of wildness, it is a demonstration of the absolute dominion of man over wild nature."

- Jay Griffiths, Wild: An Elemental Journey

17. HITTING OUT OF FAIRWAY BUNKERS

You hit your tee shot into a fairway bunker.

First, make sure you are going to clear the lip of the bunker when you decide what club you are going to use to advance the ball toward your target.

Set your feet into the sand as firmly as you can. If you hit your normal golf swing, the normal weight transfer, will force your body deeper into the sand. This increases the chances of hitting too much sand behind the ball.

Use a shallow swing sweeping the ball out with more of your arms, instead of a steep angle swing downward at the ball.

It's easier to hit a ball cleanly if you swing at it from a shallow angle with less power and focus on making good contact to pick the ball off the sand.

Use more club since you will be using your arms more and your leg action will be minimal. So, therefore you won't hit it as far as you normally do if you weren't in a fairway bunker.

*

John Daly and two of his sponsors, Tom, and Bob, were playing golf on a cloudy day. A thunderstorm suddenly moved in.

Lightning flashed repeatedly around them!

Before they could get to shelter, a bolt struck Tom right in the head and killed him instantly.

After the ambulance took Tom away, Bob said to John, "We've got to tell his wife, John. Would you be willing to go over there and tell her?"

"Why me?" said John.

"I'm just not good at it."

Daly said, "Sure, I'll go and tell her."

John left to tell the bad news to Tom's wife.

John came back to the clubhouse an hour later carrying a six pack of beer.

Bob looked at him and said, "So, did you tell her?"

"Oh yeah,' said John.

"Where did you get the six-pack?"

"Tom's wife gave it to me," said John.

"What the hell! Tom's wife gave you a six pack of beer after you told her Tom's dead?"

"Sure," says John. Bob stared at John in disbelief.

"Well," John continued, "When she answered the door, I asked her, 'Are you Tom's widow?'

"'Widow?' she said, 'No, no, you're mistaken, I'm not a widow!'

"So, I said: "I'll bet you a six pack you ARE!'"

18. HITTING ON A DOWNSLOPE

Your ball comes to rest on a downslope.

Drop your left shoulder so your shoulders are aligned parallel to the slope.

You need to make this adjustment with your shoulders since you have a good chance of mishitting or topping the ball.

One way to test if your shoulders are aligned parallel to the downward slope, is to see if you can touch your left knee with your left hand when you take your stance with your knees slightly bent.

If you can't touch your left knee, then drop your left shoulder more until you can touch you left knee with your left hand.

Use less club since the downslope will decrease the amount of loft on the club you use and the ball will travel farther.

When you make your swing at the ball, try not to lift up when you swing. Instead, focus on having your clubhead follow the downward slope on the grass.

Aim left of your target as the face of the club tends to be open when hitting on a downslope and there is a tendency for the ball to go to the left after you hit it.

"In the game of golf, the degree of adjustment to have a perfect swing is only within a few degrees."

"In life, it is very much the same; tiny changes lead to huge results."

- Anon.

19. HITTING ON AN UPSLOPE

Your ball comes to rest on an upslope.

Drop your right shoulder to align your shoulders parallel with the slope.

Focus on swinging with the upslope. That is, you align your shoulders with the upslope and swing your club head so it drops parallel with the upslope.

Use more club since the uphill slope will add more loft to the club.

Aim to the right of your target since hitting a ball on an upslope makes it difficult to rotate your body, and you will turn over your hands more and close the clubface before it hits the ball. This causes the ball to go to the left.

20. HOW TO AVOID FAT SHOTS, THIN SHOTS, AND TOPPING THE BALL

"It was a very tough 30 minutes that hopefully I will never experience again."

- Jordan Spieth, on his quadruple bogey at the 12th hole in the final round at The Masters.

A fat shot is hitting the turf behind the ball before striking the ball.

A thin shot is striking the middle of the ball with the lower part of the club.

Topping the ball is brushing the top of the ball with your club making it roll only a few yards forward.

There are several causes for these shots. Head movement is usually the main cause, but it can also be caused by too much body movement. Swaying instead of rotating your upper body, tensing up, over swinging, etc. lead to mishit shots.

The most common cure is making sure your back is straight (not curved), and stick your butt out so your upper torso swivels easier.

When you take your stance, let your arms hang down perpendicular to flat ground. Hold your chin up so your left shoulder can easily turn under your chin.

LPGA star, Paula Creamer, said, "Feel tall. Like your chest stays nice and high when you hit shots. This will help you maintain the width of your arms and prevent you from getting scoopy."

To see what she means, take your normal golf stance but focus on feeling tall. Clasp your hands together and slowly swing your arms back and forth allowing your left shoulder to move under your chin as you rotate your upper torso.

21. HAVE NO FEAR OF ANY SHOT – HOW TO HIT HIGH OR LOW TRAJECTORY APPROACH SHOTS

Dr. Alan Shapiro wrote an excellent book, "Golf's Mental Hazards." Here's an excerpt:

"Everyone has…some form of a dark side that acts out in fear, anger…. And these qualities carry over to your golf game."

"Stay positive. Know that as you are eliminating negative tendencies on the golf course, you are also working to eliminate bad qualities that hurt you in everyday life."

As you endeavor to become a better golfer, it's good to know your pursuit of playing better golf has positive benefits to your life in general.

When you maintain control over your emotions, you are practicing how to control your emotions in everyday life.

When you are facing an intimidating approach shot (whether you have to hit under an obstacle or over an obstacle), consider hitting either a low or high trajectory shot.

Low and High Trajectory Shots

If you want to hit the ball on a low trajectory, it's not that hard. Simply play the ball slightly further back in your stance.

For example, if you play a 7 iron a bit forward of the center of your stance, then if you want to hit a 7 iron on a low trajectory, play the ball in the center of your stance.

Choke down about an inch on the grip which will make the club shorter.

Then make a level swing focusing on hitting the back of the ball.

With the ball played back in your stance, and the use of a shorter club shaft length, the ball will simply come out in a low trajectory and roll further.

Don't play if off your back foot at it makes the shot more difficult.

If you're hitting to a green that's very firm or fast, or, if you're hitting to a pin tucked behind a bunker, you want to hit a high trajectory approach shot.

Play the ball more forward in your stance from where you normally play the ball.

Keep your club face open. You can do this by keeping your wrists straight at impact and use a neutral to weak grip.

Let your arms make a nice smooth swing.

*

Two golfers walk up to the Starter at an exclusive golf course. The Starter notices them and begins to negatively shake his head.

"Sorry guys, we don't have any room for two players for a tee time today."

Annoyed and disappointed, one of the golfers starts to walk back to the parking lot. The other golfer signals him to stay where he is.

"Hold on a moment. What if Jason Day and Dustin Johnson showed up to play? I'm sure you'd find a spot for them."

"Sure, of course we would," said the Starter.

"Well, they're not coming so we'll take their time."

"Stay open minded. Aim to be happy. Things aren't always as difficult as they seem."

  - Anon.

SECTION THREE: SHOTS AROUND THE GREEN

"The shorter the sand shot, the more you need to open up both your body line and club face."

- Padraig Harrington

Raymond Floyd, one of the very best at the short game said,

"As a kid in Fayetteville, N.C., I played golf all day, every day, a lot of it by myself. I spent hundreds of hours around the greens at Cape Fear Valley, the course my dad owned, hitting every shot I could think of: the one-hop-and-release, the chip that lands dead, the explosion from a bad lie."

"My advice to any golfer who wants to excel at the sport is to dedicate yourself to being good in all aspects of the game."

"Everyone, particularly young players, likes to hit the ball hard and long."

"But the real scoring part of our sport takes place from 60 yards in, so I would encourage youngsters to spend as much time learning how to chip and putt as they do with their driving."

"The finesse shots around the green and short approaches were one of the real strengths of my game, and in my prime, I felt I could outplay anyone in the game around the green,"

> *- Raymond Floyd*

22. LOB SHOT (FLOP SHOT)

"Watching Phil Mickleson play golf is like watching a drunk chase a balloon near the edge of a cliff."

- David Feherty

Phil Mickleson is a master at the flop shot.

A lob shot, or a "flop shot", sends the ball steeply into the air high and then softly stops on the green with little roll.

Lob shot are made with a lob wedge – usually having 60-64 degrees of loft.

Lob shots are used when you have little green to work with, or you want to hit the ball in a high arc over something like a small greenside bunker.

If the ball is on short grass (i.e., a tight lie vs. being propped up on thicker grass), open up your wedge so the backside of the wedge is almost lying flat on the ground.

Keep your weight forward in your stance and focus on accelerating your swing smoothly to slip the club under the ball keeping your wrists firm.

If the ball is propped up on thicker grass, use the same technique to slip the wedge under the ball, but keep your weight balanced and make your swing come into the ball at a shallow angle allowing the clubhead to slip under the ball and pop it high into the air.

Remember to use at least a 60-64-degree wedge and open the face to where the back of the clubhead is lying almost flat on the ground.

Take the club back in one piece without breaking your wrists. Then accelerate the club and slide the club face under the ball. The faster you swing, the higher the ball will rise.

23. PITCH SHOT

A pitch shot is usually played when you're within 60 yards of the green when you want to hit the ball high and land it softly on the green.

In pitching, as well as in chipping, you first select your landing area, and visualize a three-foot circle around the spot where you want the ball to land, and focus on hitting the ball to that exact area.

Your landing area determines whether you are going to hit a high pitch, a medium height pitch or a low pitch. If you want to hit it high, so the ball will roll less on the green, play the ball forward in your stance.

If you want to hit it low and have the ball run more when it hits the green, play the ball further back in your stance with your hands in front of the ball.

One way to distinguish between a pitch shot and a chip shot, is a pitch shot spends the same - or more - time in the air and less time on the ground rolling.

The chip shot is the opposite and spends more time rolling and is explained in the next chapter.

A pitch is made using a pitching wedge using your normal stance. Hold the club loosely so it will easily slide under the ball.

As you get closer to the green, you narrow your stance more, and adjust the distance you want the ball to travel by limiting the amount of backswing you take before striking the ball.

That is, for shorter distances, you may only want to make a three quarter or half of a backswing before pitching the ball.

*

"Golf is an ineffectual attempt to put an elusive ball into an obscure hole with implements ill adaptive to the purpose."

> *- Woodrow Wilson*

24. CHIPPING

Chipping is a shot used several feet off the green when you want the ball to travel only a short distance in the air, and land on the green and roll most of the distance on the green toward the pin.

You can use various clubs, but mostly irons or wedges, depending on how much distance you have between your ball and the landing area on green. The less lofted the club, the more distance the ball will roll on the green.

After you selected your landing area and the appropriate club to chip with, take several short practice swings brushing the grass feeling the texture of the grass with the clubhead.

Keep your wrists straight, and swing with your arms in line with your target. Put the ball back in your stance with your hands ahead since you want to keep the ball low, and land on your landing area and roll the rest of the way to the pin.

Place more weight on your left side. Take a slightly open stance so your arms can swing in line with your target.

Again, keep your left wrist straight and use a relaxed smooth short stroke. Focus on making good contact with the back of the ball.

"In general, the short game has been most effective for me."

"You should hit the ball according to what your mind dictates and you should visualize the shot."

"All the difficult shots are hit with the hands. I have hit shots simply by visualizing the run of the ball. I had no problem in doing this because my mind clearly indicates I cannot miss."

"It is necessary to believe in yourself to overcome any difficulties.

- *Seve Ballesteros*

25. GREENSIDE BUNKER SAND SHOT

For a normal bunker shot, use a sand wedge and put most of your weight on your left side.

Open the club face of the sand wedge. Since you are opening the club face, aim to the left of your target.

Hit one to two inches behind the ball instead of hitting the ball directly. Your clubhead enters the sand and lifts the sand *and* the ball out of the trap in one swing.

Be sure to follow through with your shot. Swing smoothly and complete your swing.

Occasionally, recreational golfers stop their swing once they feel the sand wedge enter the sand behind the ball, but finishing you swing is important to get the ball out of the sand and finish your shot with your body facing your target.

Buried "Fried Egg" Bunker Shot

If your ball is buried in the bunker, close your club face and aim it directly at the target.

A large amount of sand or damp sand will give a larger amount resistance to your club head, so you have to use a lot more force in your swing.

Swing on a steep angle down at the ball since your club head is going to dig a larger amount of sand out with the ball.

Wet Sand Bunker Shots

Wet sand offers a lot more resistance, and it's very difficult to dig a sand wedge into heavy wet sand to get the ball out.

Consider using a high lofted club like a lob wedge to skim the ball off the top of the wet sand and out of the bunker.

It's easier to skim the ball with a lob wedge off the top of wet sand, than it is trying to skim the ball off the wet sand with a sand wedge because of the large flange on the sand wedge.

Open the club face and choke down on the lob wedge. Then skim the ball of the wet sand with a log wedge hitting roughly an inch or less behind the ball.

*

One for the clubhouse bar:

Four guys are sitting in the clubhouse bar when another member walks in with his pet monkey.

He orders a drink, but while he's drinking it, the monkey is jumping all over the place, eating everything behind the bar, chips off the table, scraps on the floor. Then the monkey jumps on the pool table and swallows the cue ball.

The bartender screams at the guy, "Your monkey just ate the cue ball off the pool table – whole!"

"Very sorry," says the guy. "He eats everything in the universe, the little bastard. Please put all he's eaten, and any other damage on my account. I'll pay for everything."

The member finishes his drink, signs his account for the damages and leaves.

Two weeks later, the same foursome is in the bar having a drink after just finishing their round, and the same member walks in again with his monkey.

He orders a drink and the monkey starts running all over the place again and finds a maraschino cherry by the bar. The monkey takes the cherry and sticks it up his ass, then pulls it out, and eats it!

The bartender almost vomits and says, "Did you see what the little bastard just did? That's sickening!"

"Yeah," replied the member. "He still eats everything in the universe, but ever since he swallowed the cue ball, he measures it first."

26. FRINGE SHOTS

TEXAS WEDGE

If your ball is off the green on the fringe, consider keeping things simple and use your "Texas Wedge" aka your putter, to putt the ball over the fringe and onto the green to the pin.

You could chip it, but using your putter is simple and may be easier if the fringe is smooth.

You hit the ball as you would a putt, but only hit it a little harder to get the ball through the longer grass on the fringe and to roll freely to the pin once it reaches the green.

THREE-WOOD OFF THE COLLAR

If your ball comes to rest on the fringe with high blades of grass directly behind the back of the ball, consider using your three-wood, five-wood, or hybrid to hit the grass and back of the ball using a putting stroke.

Choke down on the shaft to increase your chances of making good contact with the grass and back of the ball.

These clubs usually get through the long grass a lot easier and increase your percentages in hitting it closer to the pin.

HYBRID CHIP

While most golfers use a wedge if you have ten or more feet of fringe to get through plus a lot of green to work with, you might want to consider chipping with a hybrid instead of a wedge.

Choke down on the hybrid and play the ball back in your stance to increase your chances of making good contact with the ball.

The loft of the hybrid will get the ball briefly up in the air and bouncing low and rolling over the fringe and onto the green toward the pin.

Hitting balls off the fringe and onto the green with these clubs takes a lot of concentration and feel.

Like most anything, practicing shots around the green will make you better at using these as well as all of the greenside shots.

If concentration over these shots get to you, keep in mind, golf is a sport to be enjoyed. Relax, and don't be afraid to laugh.

"If you can't laugh at yourself, then how can you laugh at anybody else?"

"I think people see the human side of you when you do that."

> *- Payne Stewart*

27. CHIPPING FROM A DOWNHILL OR UPHILL SLOPE ONTO A FAST GREEN

Your ball comes to rest on a steep downhill slope just off the green and you want to chip it.

You pick your landing spot and visualize a one to two-foot circle around your landing spot.

It's best not to try and chip the ball high in the air (since the ground is already going downhill, the ball will roll quite a bit if it lands on a downslope). Visualize chipping it on a low trajectory.

Take a wide stance so you'll be better able to keep your balance, especially on a very steep downhill slope.

Angle your shoulders to match the contour of the slope. Again, a way to check if your shoulders match the downhill slope is to see if you can reach your left kneecap with your left hand.

Take a few practice swings brushing the grass. Your practice swings need to brush the grass without stubbing the club into the ground and swing smoothly parallel with the slope of the hill.

Take note of where the club brushes the grass and address the ball in your stance at that point.

Hit the shot and follow through chipping the ball to your landing area.

Tiger Woods uses sand wedge to put reverse spin on the ball to keep if from rolling too fast on a downhill chip.

For an uphill slope, you can use these same techniques but when doing your practice swings, note where the club brushes the upsloping ground and address the ball accordingly to avoid stubbing your club into the ground.

The uphill slope will add more loft to your club to make the chip go higher in the air, so you need to make an adjustment for this when you select your landing area.

"One of the easiest shots in golf is chipping. It should be the easiest. It's like throwing a ball or pitching pennies. It's easy. And I struggle with that, and the struggle is all mental."

- Nick Saban

28. THE EASIEST SHOT IN GOLF

You are playing with the club pro and you tee off on the first hole which is a long 200+ yard par three.

You hit your tee shot just in front of a large, deep greenside sand trap. You now must hit your ball a short way over the large, deep trap to an elevated green.

The club pro hits to the green and you're away.

You get ready to hit your shot when the club pro says, "Hey, that's the easiest shot in golf!"

"What?"

The club pro smiles and says, "You're going to hit your next shot into the bunker. That's the easiest shot in golf!"

You then chunk your shot into the bunker. "Very funny!"

As you walk into the trap, the pro says, "Do you know what the second easiest shot in golf is?"

"What?"

The pro smiles again and says, "You're going to leave your next shot in the bunker."

It's feels intimidating at times to chip from a tight lie over a deep trap. But, there is an easy method. Play the ball back in your stance using a high lofted club. Your hands should be in front of the ball, and most of your weight is forward on your left side. This set-up helps you strike the ball first and not flub it into the bunker.

Take the wrist action out of the shot, and keeping your wrists straight, take an easy relaxed swing half swing. Allow the loft of the club to raise the ball over the bunker, onto the green and rolling toward the pin.

There really is no "Easiest shot in golf." Every golfer is an individual and has a shot he likes and does easily. We all know, golfers vary in ability, and shots that are easy for some and hard for others.

Tom Watson said his easiest shot in golf was a shot he learned from Ray Floyd - chipping with a putting stroke.

Golf without bunkers and hazards would be tame and monotonous. So would life.

- B. C. Forbes

29. THE DELICATE DROP SHOT

A drop shot is used when your ball is in deep, heavy grass around the green.

If you were further away from the green in heavy grass you most likely would use force and hit the ball out of the heavy grass.

A drop shot is used when you want to get the ball out of the heavy grass near the green and rolling on the green - *delicately.*

Since the grass is thick and heavy, if you tried to make a full smooth swing at the ball, you risk stubbing the shot with the heavy grass catching the club head and leaving the ball in the rough.

If you took a full powerful swing at the ball, you risk fully catching the ball and hitting it too far.

To do a (delicate pop-out) drop shot, take a high lofted club like a 60-degree wedge and chop down quickly at the back of the ball with it. You need to accelerate the club downward at a steep angle directly behind the ball.

The ball should pop out on to the green and roll toward your target with little or no spin on the ball.

Quick Drill: Put 10 balls near the edge of the practice green in deep, thick grass. Chop down on the back of the ball popping it out and rolling on the green. See how close you can get it to the pin.

Put 10 balls in the same heavy rough but try to force the ball out by chipping. See which method works better for you.

30. BUMP AND RUN SHOT

There's is a well-known saying in golf, "Your worst pitch isn't going to be better than your worst chip," and, there is a lesser known saying, "You don't have to put the ball in the air if you don't have to since there's no pictures on scorecards."

A bump and run shot is a low shot used about 40 yards or less to the green.

Use a bump and run shot when there is a clear path to the pin without any obstacles or hazards in your way.

Take a narrow stance, play the ball back in your stance with your hands slightly ahead.

You hit the shot with an iron of your choice planning to carry the ball halfway in the air on a low trajectory to the pin and allowing the ball to run on the ground the other half way to the pin.

If the green is small and you have a clear path to the pin, it's easier to judge the distance by running the ball up on a low trajectory in this manner than to hit it high in the air and have the ball possibly roll of the side or back of the green.

"Golf is like acting in that both require concentration and relaxation at the same time. In acting, you can't push emotion. You have to let it rise from you naturally. Same thing in golf. You just let it happen and enjoy the smooth swing."

- Jane Seymour, Actress

Interesting comparison by Jane Seymour who starred as a James Bond girl in "Live and Let Die" and who is an avid golfer.

A bump and run shot is not a glamourous shot, but if it gets the job done and you feel relaxed about using a bump and run, then go for it and use it more often when the opportunity is there.

31. HIT INTO THE BANK SHOT

The bank shot is a shot played when your ball is close to the green but there is a bank or a berm you must hit the ball over to get the ball on the green without rolling far on the green.

If there isn't much green to work with, chances are if you chip it up in the air and land it on the green, the ball might roll further away from the pin than you are already.

You could try a flop shot instead of the bank shot. The bank shot is an alternative to a flop shot. Choose whichever shot you have the most confidence in.

To do a bank shot, pitch the ball directly into the face of the bank. When the ball hits the face of the bank, it will slow the speed of the ball down, and the ball will pop up in the air and slowly roll onto the green near the pin.

Play the ball back in your stance and use a narrow stance with your hands ahead of the ball.

DRILL: Hit Balls into the Bank

Hitting a ball into a bank takes practice to get a good feel for this shot and few golfers practice ever practice it. If the practice area has a chipping green with a bank, drop ten practice balls and hit them into the side of the bank trying to stop the ball within 10 feet from where the green begins, i.e. imagine you only have about 10 feet of green to work with.

Try using different irons and see how many balls you keep within 10 feet.

"Golf is a game to teach you about the messages from within."

"It's about the subtle voices of your body and mind."

"Once you understand these voices,"

"You can more clearly see...the ways in which your approach to the game reflects your entire life."

"Nowhere does a man go so naked."

- Michael Murphy, From "Golf in the Kingdom".

Thank you for reading "Golf Shots" We hope this book makes golf more enjoyable for you.

Above all, have fun playing golf and enjoy all your adventures!

If you liked reading our book, please be kind and give it a review so others can find it.

For putting techniques, you might like to read our book on Putting Techniques,

<u>"Golf Putting Techniques from Golfing Greats: Proven Putting Techniques from Tiger, Rory, Jason Day, Jordan Spieth, and Others."</u>

Team at Golfwell's Other Books

Golf Putting Techniques from Golfing Greats: Proven Putting Techniques from Tiger, Rory, Jason Day, Jordan Spieth, and Others

Team at Golfwell's Other Books

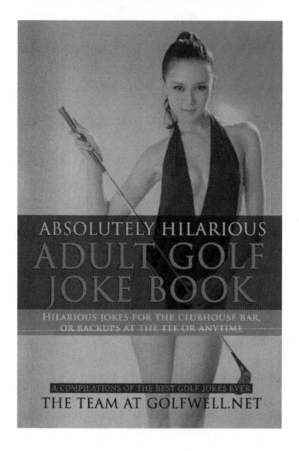

Absolutely Hilarious Adult Golf Joke Book

Team at Golfwell's Other Books

Fascinating Golf Stories and More Hilarious Adult Golf Jokes

(Second in the Golfwell Adult Joke Book Series)

Team at Golfwell's Other Books

Golf Driving Techniques from Golfing Greats and Golf Stories

Team at Golfwell's Other Books

Why Do Little Fat Ladies Beat Me at Golf?

How to Correct Common Golf Mistakes

Team at Golfwell's Other Books

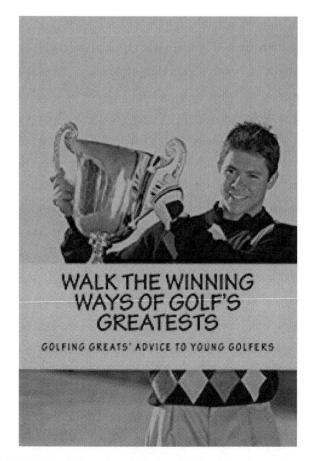

Walk the Winning Ways of Golf's Greatests

Team at Golfwell's Other Books

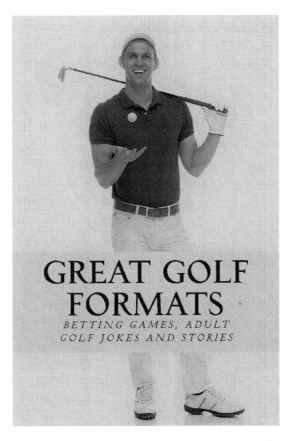

Great Golf Formats: Betting Games and More Hilarious Adult Golf Jokes and Stories and Third in the Golfwell Adult Joke Book Series

A final message to you from The Team at Golfwell:

We hope this book made golf more enjoyable for you.

If you have any suggestions for other shot techniques to build your shot arsenal, we'd like to hear from you.

Above all, have fun playing golf and enjoy all your adventures!

If you liked our book, please give it a review.

Thank you for reading and best to you!

Info@TeamGolfwell.com

<u>More about the Team at Golfwell</u>

Made in the USA
Middletown, DE
27 December 2023

46850684R10071